Before &After

You Fall In Love

by
Victoria Brown and Allan Chochinov

ST. MARTIN'S PRESS • NEW YORK

BEFORE & AFTER™—YOU FALL IN LOVE

ISBN: 0-312-95390-9

Before & After is the exclusive trademark of
Victoria Brown and Allan Chochinov

Book and cover design: Victoria Brown and Allan Chochinov
Authors' photos: John Glembin

Printed in the United States of America

St. Martin's Paperbacks edition / February 1995

10 9 8 7 6 5 4 3 2 1

Before

Twice a night

After

Twice a month

Before

"She says she loves the way
I take control of a situation."

After

*"She called me a controlling,
manipulative egomaniac."*

Before

Lucy
&
Ricky

After

*Fred
&
Ethel*

Before

"He never does anything without asking me first."

After

"He never does anything without asking me first."

Before

Saturday Night Fever

After

Monday Night Football

Before

"He makes me feel
like a million dollars!"

After

*"If I had a dime for every
stupid thing he's done…"*

Before

"Don't Stop!"

After

don't start.

Before

The Sound of Music

After

The Sounds of Silence

Before

"He always wants to do it
with the lights on!"

After

*"He always wants to do it
with the lights OFF."*

Before

"Is that all you're having?"

After

"Maybe you should just order a salad, honey."

Before

Wheel Of Fortune

After

Jeopardy!

Before

"It's like I'm living in a dream!"

After

"It's like he's living in a dorm."

Before

$60.00 / doz.

After

$1.95 / stem

Before

"I love it when you talk dirty."

After

#@/ΣX*!

Before

"Every morning I wake up
and see his face!"

After

*"Every morning I wake up
and see his face."*

Before

TURBO CHARGED!

After

jump start.

Before

"We agree on everything!"

After

"Doesn't she have a mind of her own?"

Before

Victoria's Secret

After

Fruit of the Loom

Before

"He calls me his 'little princess'!"

After

"Last night he called me a princess*!"*

Before

charming and noble

After

Chernobyl

Before

"He makes me wonder
what I would do without him."

After

*"He makes me wonder
what I would do without him."*

Before

feathers and handcuffs

After

ball and chain

Before

idol

After

idle

Before

"I like a woman with curves."

After

"I never said you were fat."

Before

"He's completely lost without me!"

After

"Why won't he ever ask for directions?"

Before

"I just want to spend quiet evenings with you at home."

After

"Can't we ever go out?"

Before

Erotic

After

neurotic

Before

Roses are red
And violets are blue

After

*I never promised
A rose garden for you*

Before

"We never get out of bed!"

After

"HE never gets out of bed."

Before

"What are you thinking?"

After

"What could you have possibly *been thinking?!"*

Before

1-800-ROMANCE

After

1-900-REALITY

Before

"I can't say enough
good things about him."

After

*"HE can't say enough
good things about him."*

Before

Time stood still

After

This relationship is going nowhere.

Before

"I love it when he misbehaves!"

After

"He acts like a child."

Before

croissant & cappuccino

After

bagel & instant

Before

"He always wants to know where I am."

After

"He always wants to know where I am!"

Before

"I've never done *that* before."

After

"I'll never do that again."

Before

blind

After

nearsighted

Before

"You look so seductive in black."

After

"All your clothes are so depressing."

Before

iambic pentameter

After

blank verse

Before

"And then he reached over
and fed me chocolate pudding off of his finger!"

After

*"He can't stop
playing with his food."*

Before

right of way

After

yield

Before

"I'm having such a hard time
getting him to put his defenses down."

After

"I'm having such a hard time getting him to put the seat down."

Before

I - ♥ - U

After

R-E-S-P-E-C-T

Before

"I can't get him out of my mind."

After

"I can't get him out of the house."

Before

oysters!

After

fishsticks.

Before

"And he drives the most
adorable little car!"

After

*"Well, actually, we're thinking of investing
in something a little more upscale."*

Before

"She's always calling me just to say she loves me!"

After

"She's always calling me."

Before

"Last night we did it on the couch!"

After

"Last night I slept on the couch."

Before

"I can't believe I ended up
with someone like you."

After

*"I can't believe I ended up
with someone like you."*

Before

passion

After

ration

Before

Once Upon A Time

After

The end.

When rock'n'roll
becomes rock-a-bye-baby…

Before&After
Your New Baby

"Pampers
saved my life."

"Disposable diapers
are killing the planet."

Victoria Brown   Allan Chochinov

Before&After
SERIES

Before &After Your New Baby

by Victoria Brown and Allan Chochinov

"We've read every baby book.
We're completely prepared for this."

Your bundle of joy is on the way. You watch the neo-natal crowd zipping down the sidewalks and think, "They look so happy. This is going to be the most fulfilling experience of my life." You're going to do all the wonderful things that *your* mother did (and maybe make an adjustment or two along the way). Baby, it's only a Lamaze class away.

"Nothing in the world could have prepared us for this."

Wake up and smell the formula. Now you're taking orders from an infant-tesimal boss who doesn't speak your language, expects you to be on-call 24-hours-a-day, and shows gratitude by spitting up on your new shirt! Life will never be the same and neither will your wardrobe. Mama said there'd be days like this.

BEFORE & AFTER YOUR NEW BABY
Victoria Brown & Allan Chochinov
95339–9 _____ $5.99 U.S. _____ $6.99 CAN.

Publishers Book and Audio Mailing Service
P.O. Box 120159, Staten Island, NY 10312-0004
Please send me the book(s) I have checked above. I am enclosing $_____ (Please add $2.00 for the first book, and $0.75 for each additional book to cover postage and handling. Send check or money order only – no CODs) or charge my VISA, MASTER-CARD, DISCOVER or AMERICAN EXPRESS card.

Card number _____

Expiration date _____ Signature _____

Name _____

Address _____

City _____ State/Zip _____

Please allow six weeks for delivery. Prices subject to change without notice. Payment in U.S. funds only. New York residents add applicable sales tax.

BEFORE 9/94